# A Cup of Butter

## A book by RL Lane

*Dedicated to…*

A cup of butter

2 tbsp sugar

No…

This is not a recipe

It is a flower

Little yellow flowers

I see them everywhere this year

It must mean something

Someone must have sent them to me

The little yellow cups…*buttercups.*

I knew it was a special drawing, partially because it was a flower, but I had to take it apart to see what it contained...

The center…

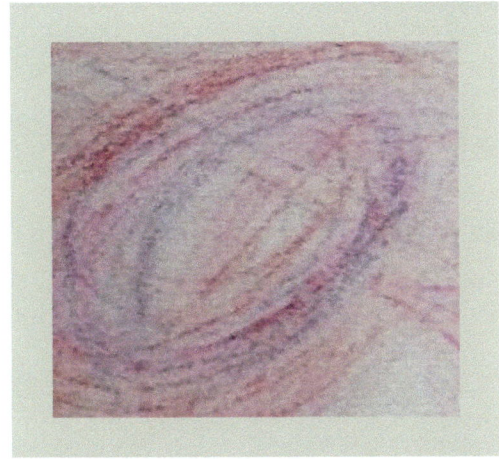

*Do you see the cross in the middle of the flower…slanted to the right…*

Do you see the angel…

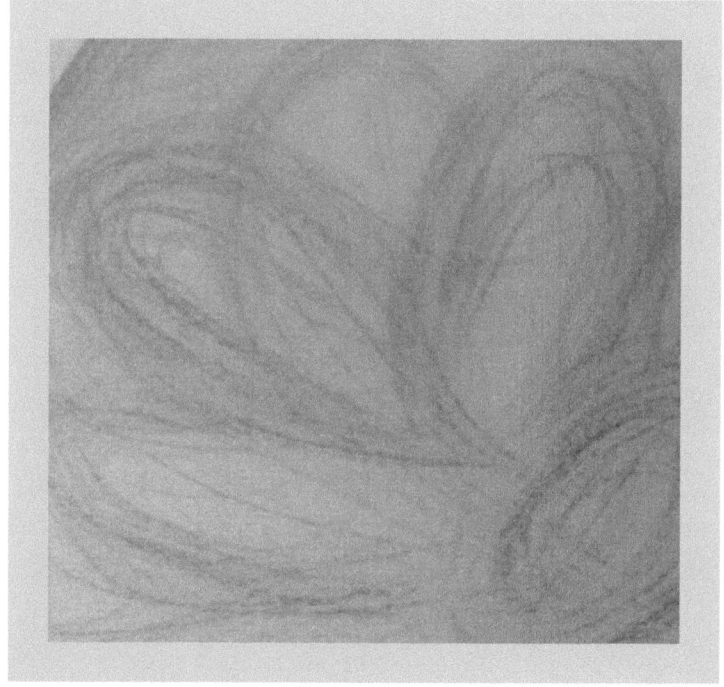

*She is wearing a hood…floating through the night…*

Do you see it transforming before your eyes…

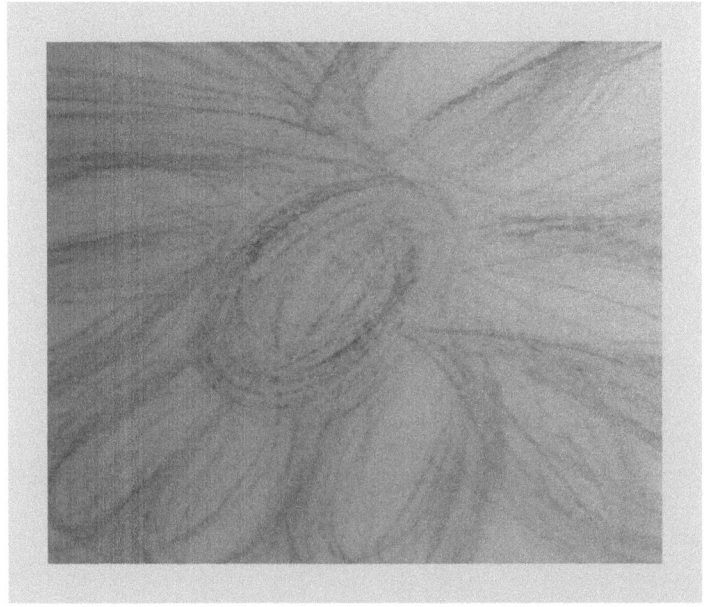

*Turning, churning, like mixing, making the butter…*

How exactly do you make butter?

Pour a pint of heavy cream into a jar with a tight-fitting lid
Once the butter has solidified, pour off the buttermilk
And then you will have…

Old-fashioned butter
No churning required


*Oh.  I think they are saying the churning was hard*

*The old-fashioned way*

A lot of labor went into the things they loved…

We no longer have the labor

For the same things we love

*Oh. Are they saying…*

Someone recently said to me "don't sweat the small things"…

I think they were mistaken

I think they meant to say to sweat them

Do care about the little things…


The tiniest part on a big plane

The smallest person on the team…

I think it was just supposed to be…

"Don't care about the things that are not important"


But so many things are important

How do we find the time for them all?

How do we pick and choose?

What, what, and when?

It is important to work hard, to study hard, to help others…

Go here go there spend your time this way and that way…

Do do do do dododo…until you feel like a dodo bird…

*Oh.  That is what they are saying…*

When that happens…when you become the dodo bird…that is when you have gone too far…extended yourself too much…and it is time to come back…

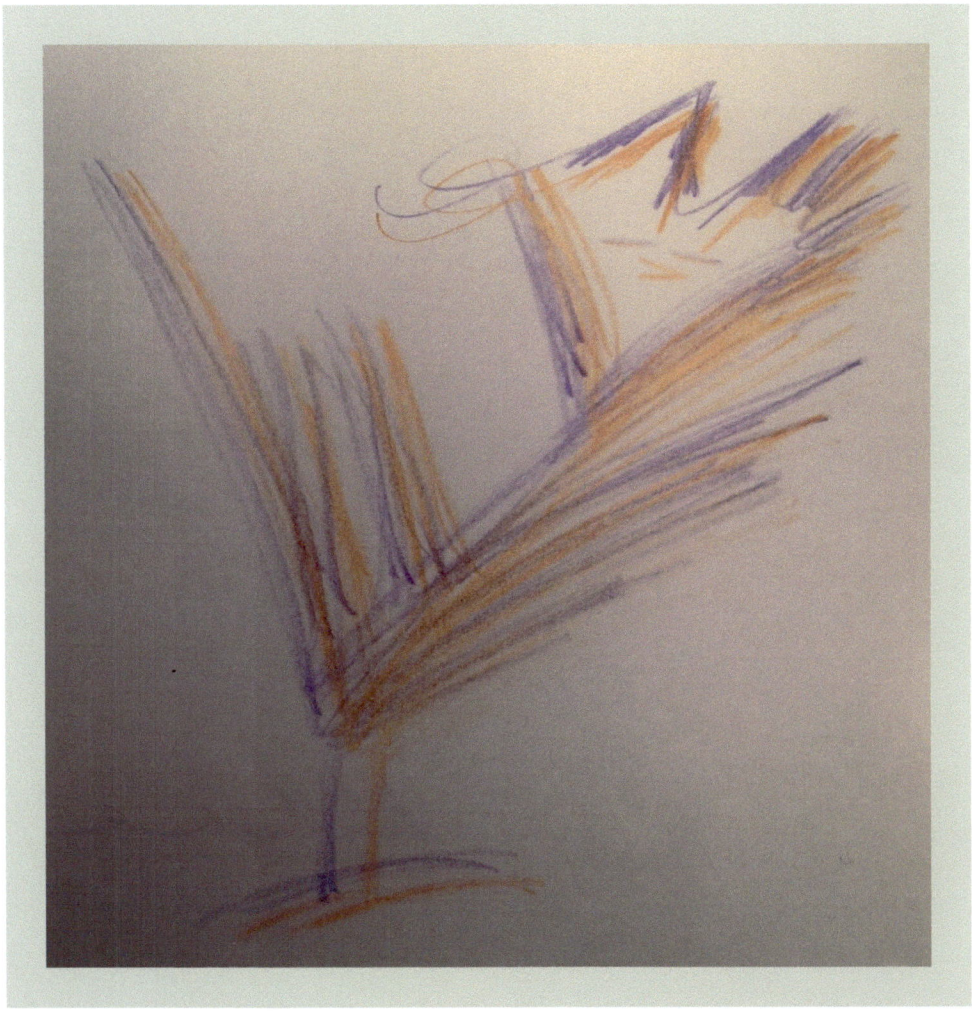

...back to the beginning.  Just remember the beginning...

The first day you were born…

You had a whole life ahead of you

Day 1 had just begun…Inning Number 1

You weren't expected to do anything

You just had to "be"

Remember that day…

Oh.  You can't remember that day

So remember what that day meant…

It meant you were given life.

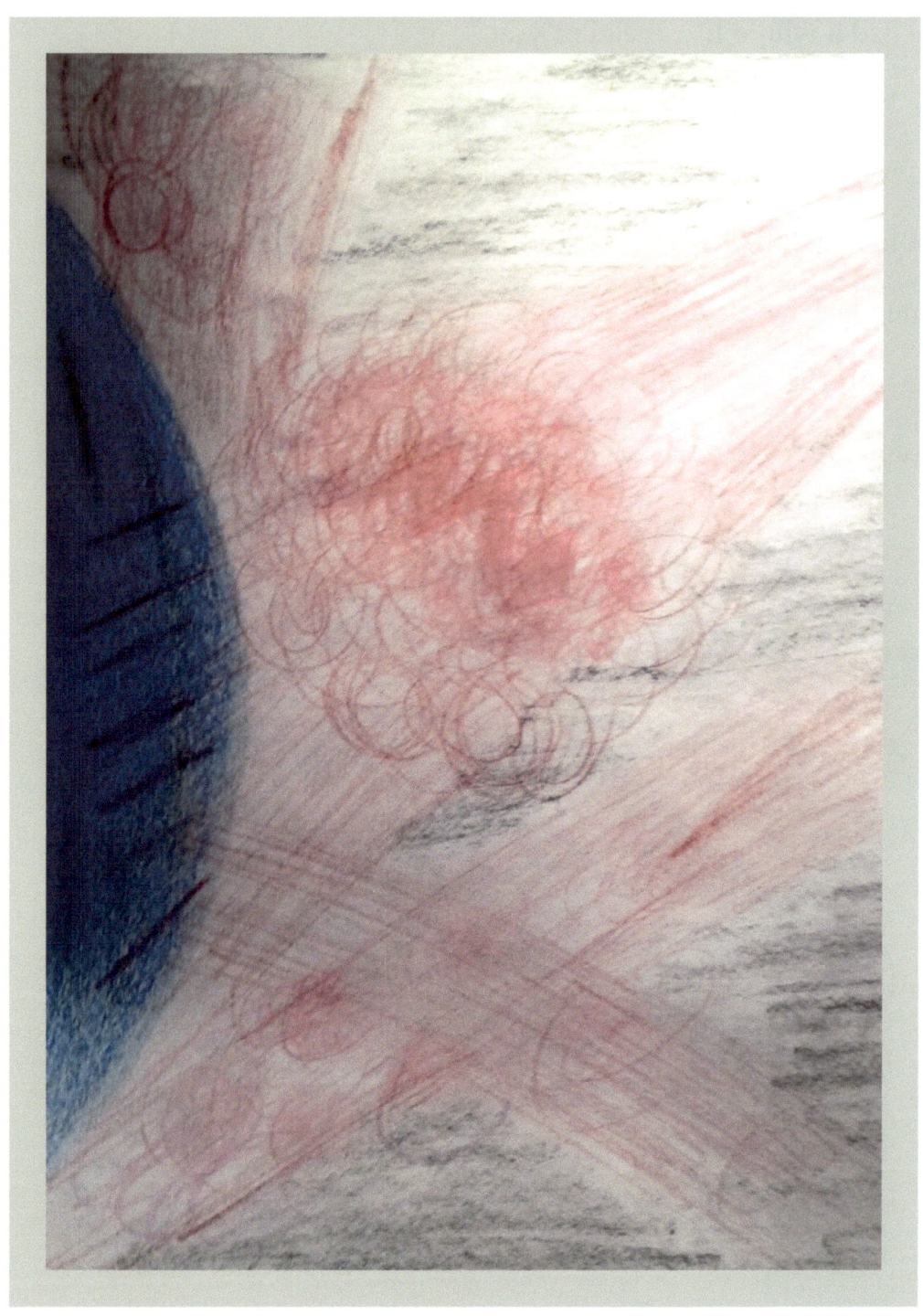

For whatever reason, you were given it and it is your life...

You pick and choose how you spend your time. Maybe that is why we have birthdays. So we can think about how we spent our time the last year…

No one has all the answers, and really we are the only ones who can answer how we should be spending our time…

But I do know it is important

to acknowledge a person's birthday

It is true it comes only once every 365 days

except in a leap year…

When the next one comes, think about when you opened your eyes for the first time…

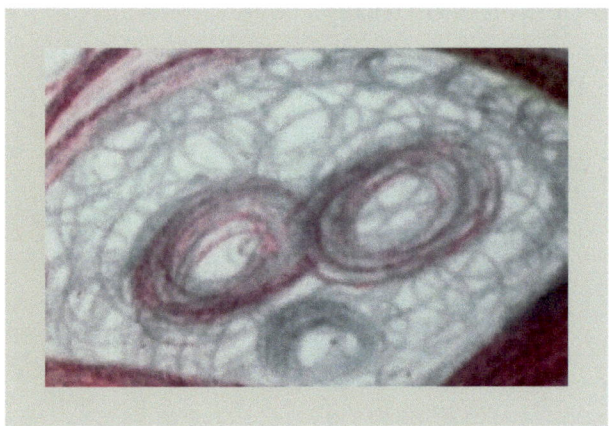

Looked around for the first time

I wondered what your brain thought

The first time you looked at your parents

Or the first time you looked at a doctor or nurse…

*Did your eyes grow to see the world around us…or did they shut somewhere along the way…*

I do know it is important to say it…

"Happy Birthday"

It is important to send a card

A physical card…an e-card…or

A card


Within


A


Book…

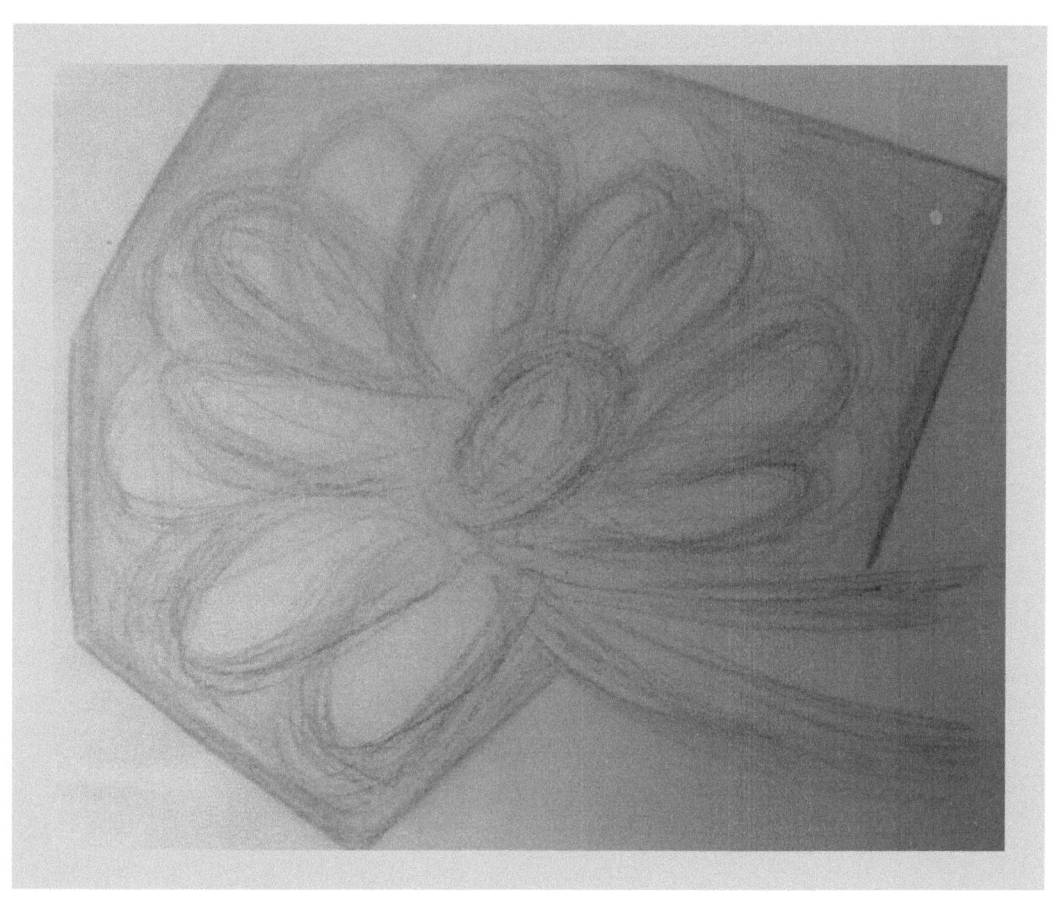

*Something about this reminds me of home plate...*

It is funny that I recently had a dream about the person who I wrote this book for…

It was a dream of her pulling the string on a flower

And the whole thing unraveled

I had drawn the flower card back on May 16 of 2015

It has a flower with a string…


In the dream, she pulled the string and the whole flower

Unraveled

Unfolded

Disassembled


She won't have to worry

This flower has no real strings

That will destroy it


It is safe on the card

In this book

To see forever


To remember forever…

The real message

The important one

That is being sent

Which is simply…

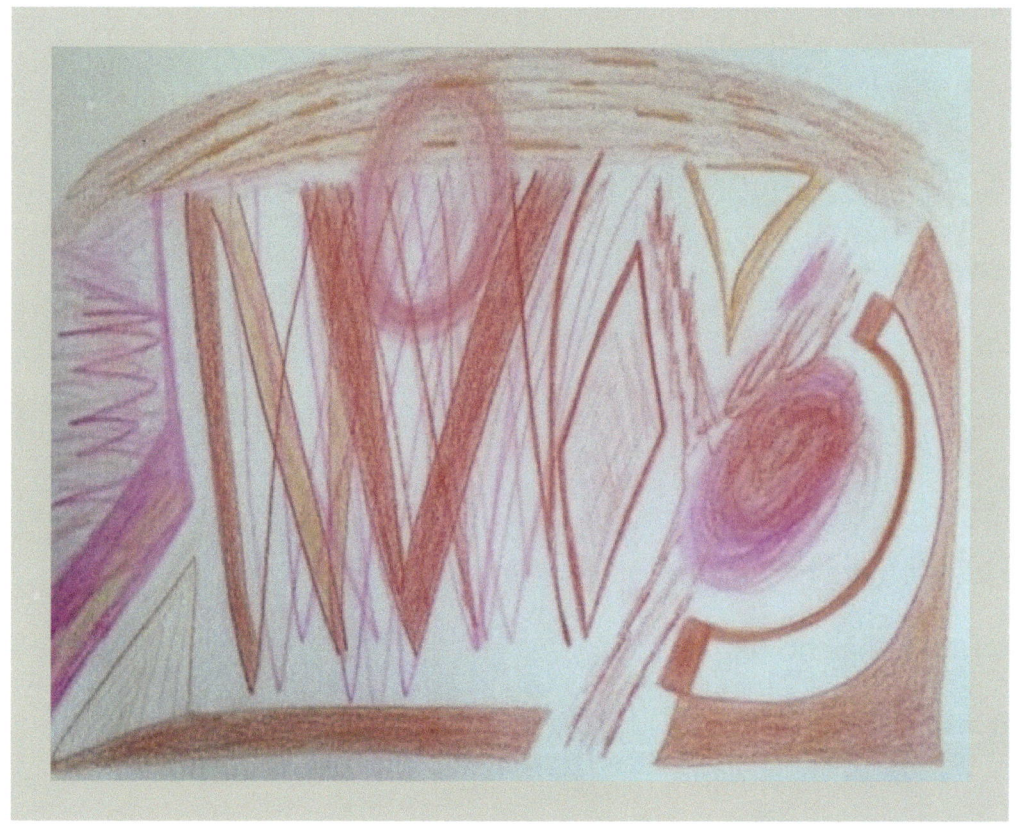

*Dedicated to…*

# About the Author and *Illustrator*

RL Lane has published the EcarreT series and a collection of art books featuring the illustrations throughout the books. The series begins with "Chapel Street Signs"…

…unexplained connections that challenge us to beli ve. A woman, a Dad a Doctor, a cat and mouse, a horse and tale tell their stories. "Do you beli ve in spirits?" I asked my friend. "Well look", he said, "I believe there are things that cannot be explained…" Oh. Plus, hear ov a Mom's battle with her struggle to connect to the woman…her little girl.

*Welcome to EcarreT…a world*
*Where everyone cares*
*Why did I have to create it in…*

A fiction fantasy world?

You may already know why, but you will see regardless of what you believe as a girl's journey of love and faith on her "Touring Machine" take her on the best journey of her mundane life. A life well on its way takes a turn in a direction that could've never been seen or even dreamed…

The author can be contacted at:

RosaLeeeLane@gmail.com
www.Amazon.com/author/readrllane

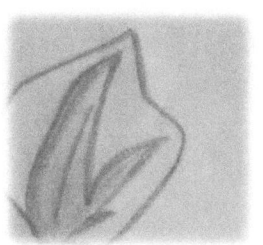

ISBN: 1514711540
ISBN-13: 978-1514711545